The Story of LONDON

Richard Brassey

Dolphin Paperbacks

For
Judith Elliott,
simply the best

First published in Great Britain 2004
by Orion Children's Books
a division of the Orion Publishing Group Ltd
Orion House
5 Upper St Martin's Lane
London WC2H 9EA

A catalogue record for this book is available from the British Library.

Printed in Italy

ISBN 1 84255 222 8

Three hundred years ago the skeleton of a woolly mammoth was found under the ground in the middle of London.

At the time people were puzzled about how it had got there. We now know that early Londoners also included hippos, crocodiles and elephants. There were once even lions in Trafalgar Square. (Of course, Trafalgar Square wasn't there then.)

We know too that Stone Age peoples lived in the area as long as half a million years ago.

But it was only after the last Ice Age, 12,000 years ago, that people like us arrived. They began to use bronze and then the latest iron tools. It was quite a busy place, but everybody lived in scattered settlements. There was no London town before the arrival of the Romans.

The first Roman invasion of Britain was led by Julius Caesar. He didn't stay long. He did defeat a large army of natives in the London area and it's just possible he built a pontoon bridge where London Bridge stands today.

LONDINIUM – THE OBVIOUS PLACE

It was another hundred years before the Romans moved in properly. In 43 AD the Emperor Claudius arrived. His army included elephants, which terrified the Britons. Claudius made the old tribal centre of Colchester the capital, because Londinium hadn't been built yet.

But within fifteen years Londinium had grown into a bustling place and was just getting going when . . . disaster struck. A tribal queen named Boudica led a revolt against the Romans and burnt the whole place to the ground.

IT WAS FULL OF TRADERS, A FAMOUS CENTRE OF COMMERCE.

TACITUS
Roman historian writing in 100 AD

BOUDICA

When Queen Boudica's husband died in 60 AD, the Romans decided to take over his lands. She was furious. With the help of other tribes she attacked Colchester and Londinium. The Roman legions, who were busy in Wales, raced back and soon defeated her, but by then Londinium was just a pile of ash. Legend says Boudica is buried under King's Cross Station, but nobody really knows her fate.

Boudica's revolt was the first of many catastrophes in London's history, but the city bounced back, as it always would. A proper bridge was built and by 100 AD it had become the capital of Roman Britain.

Twenty years later most of it was accidentally burnt to the ground again, and again soon rebuilt. Later still quite a few Londiniumers simply left. We don't know why. Their houses fell into ruins and seem to have been replaced by vegetable gardens.

THAT'S A GOOD SIZE CARROT, LONGINUS.
YOU SHOULD SEE MY ONIONS!

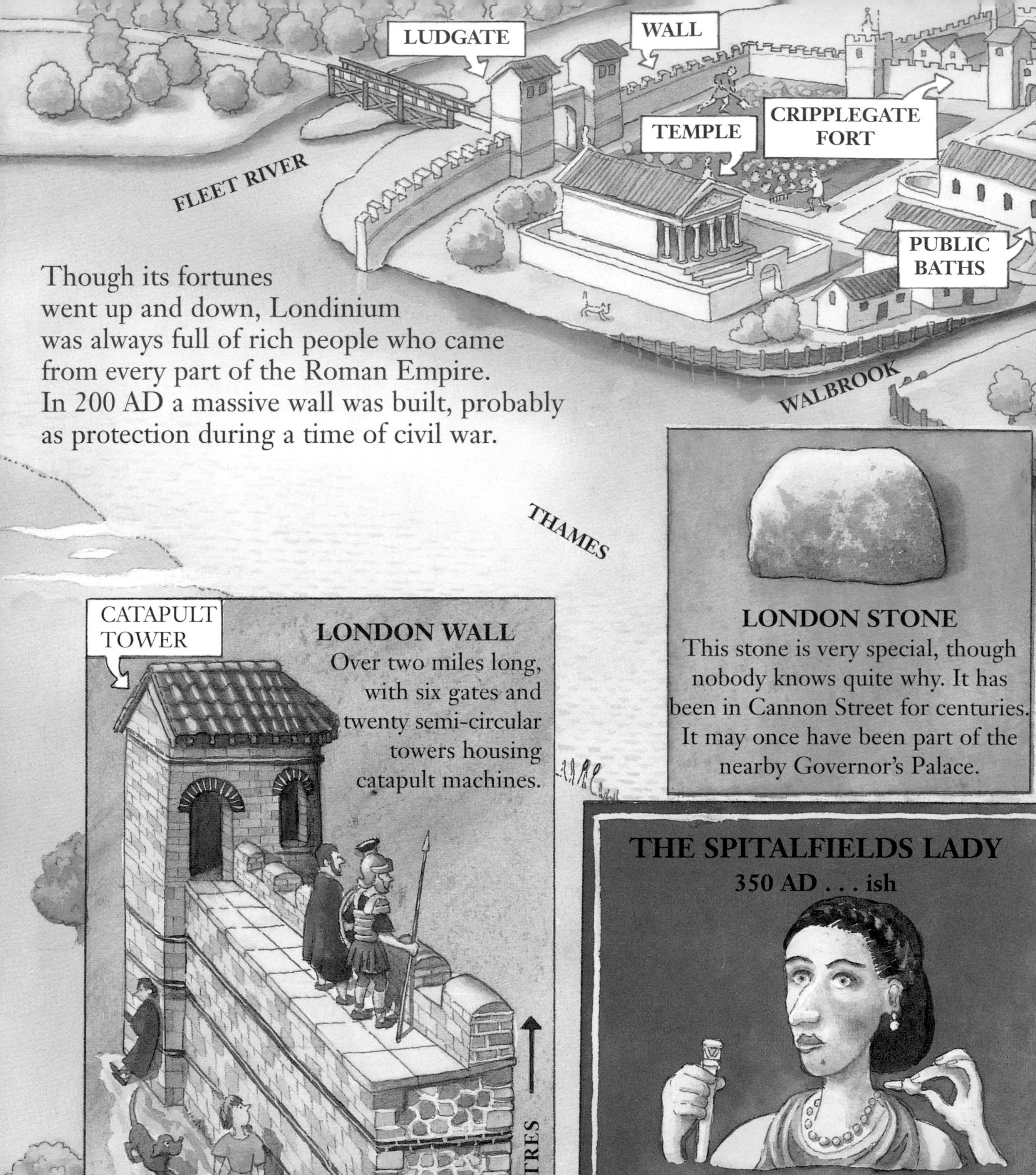

Though its fortunes went up and down, Londinium was always full of rich people who came from every part of the Roman Empire. In 200 AD a massive wall was built, probably as protection during a time of civil war.

LONDON WALL

Over two miles long, with six gates and twenty semi-circular towers housing catapult machines.

Only a few small bits of wall remain today.

LONDON STONE

This stone is very special, though nobody knows quite why. It has been in Cannon Street for centuries. It may once have been part of the nearby Governor's Palace.

THE SPITALFIELDS LADY

350 AD . . . ish

This young woman's skeleton, dressed in silk with gold threads, was found in a stone coffin at Spitalfields. Her family were probably rich newcomers from Spain. A model of her head is in the Museum of London. She is the first Londoner whose face we can see.

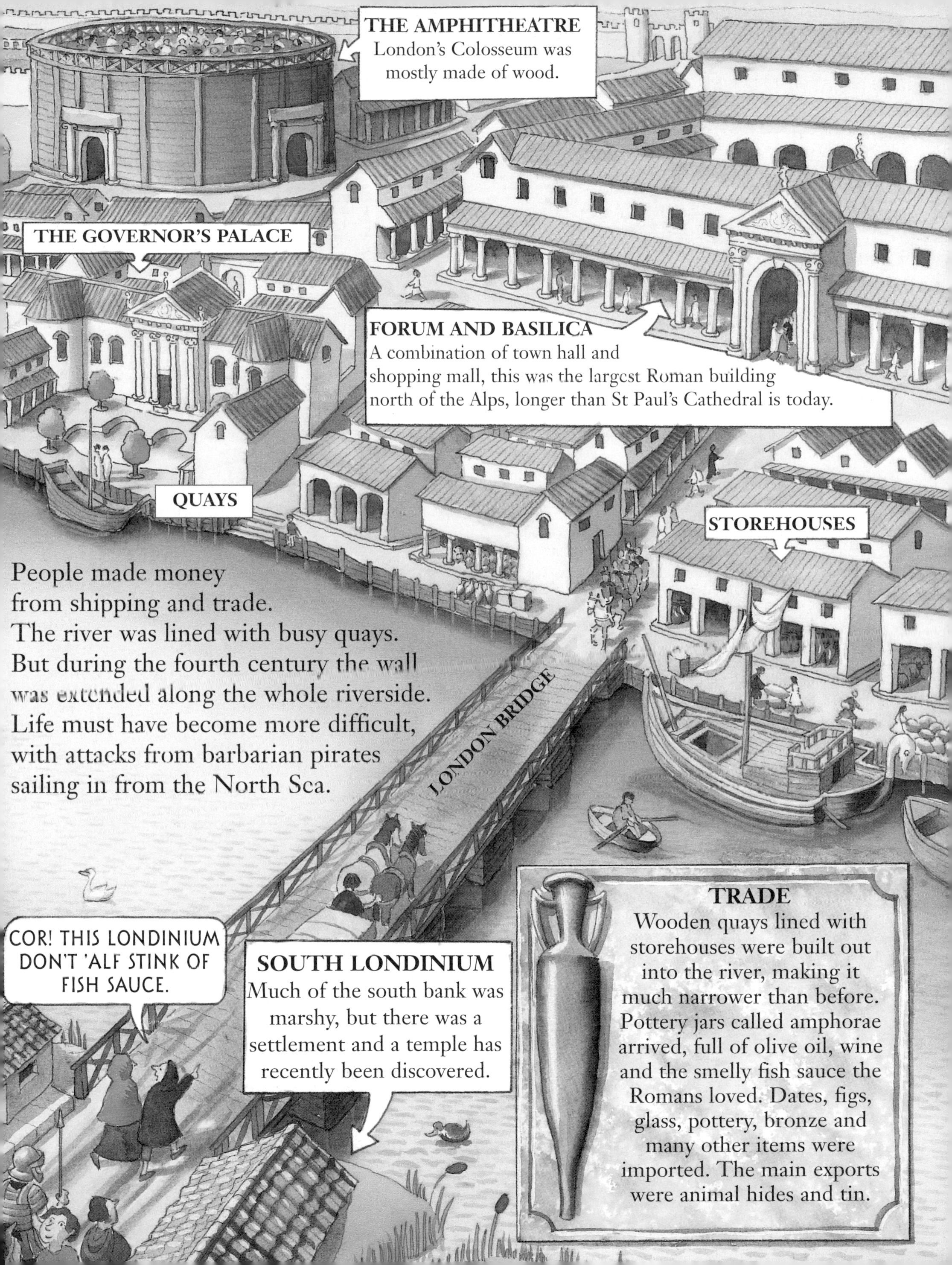
THE AMPHITHEATRE
London's Colosseum was mostly made of wood.
THE GOVERNOR'S PALACE
FORUM AND BASILICA
A combination of town hall and shopping mall, this was the largest Roman building north of the Alps, longer than St Paul's Cathedral is today.
QUAYS
STOREHOUSES
People made money from shipping and trade. The river was lined with busy quays. But during the fourth century the wall was extended along the whole riverside. Life must have become more difficult, with attacks from barbarian pirates sailing in from the North Sea.
LONDON BRIDGE
COR! THIS LONDINIUM DON'T 'ALF STINK OF FISH SAUCE.
SOUTH LONDINIUM
Much of the south bank was marshy, but there was a settlement and a temple has recently been discovered.
TRADE
Wooden quays lined with storehouses were built out into the river, making it much narrower than before. Pottery jars called amphorae arrived, full of olive oil, wine and the smelly fish sauce the Romans loved. Dates, figs, glass, pottery, bronze and many other items were imported. The main exports were animal hides and tin.

As the Roman Empire came more and more under attack from barbarians, the legions were needed closer to home. The last ones left Britain in 410.

LONDON LEGENDS
History got a bit muddled after the Romans left. Some strange legends grew up.
NEW TROY
London was founded by a Trojan called Brutus, after the fall of Troy.
It was named after King Lud. Until 1760 there was a statue of Lud on Ludgate, one of the city gates.
Two giants called Gog and Magog guarded the two hills of London. Their grandfather was the Roman Emperor Diocletian.
People believed these stories, but there's no evidence that any of these characters ever existed, except Diocletian!
LUNDENWIC IS A MARKET OF MANY PEOPLES COMING BY LAND AND SEA.
VENERABLE BEDE
English historian writing in 730 AD
ALDWYCH
means 'old market'. This is one of the few clues that Lundenwic ever existed.
FLEET RIVER
LUDGATE

Not long afterwards Londinium was overrun by Saxons. The Saxons were farmers and country dwellers. The city meant nothing to them and within a few years it had become a ruined ghost town. Instead, a settlement of wooden buildings called Lundenwic grew up along the river to the west. In time it became a busy port.

But Lundenwic was defenceless when first Vikings and then Danes began to raid along the English coast. In 886 the Saxon King Alfred sensibly moved the population within the safety of the Roman walls again. London has never looked back.

ALFRED THE GREAT
849-899

BURNING CAKES ISN'T ALL I DID!

The only English king ever to be called 'Great', Alfred united the English against the Danes, reoccupied the city and rebuilt the walls.

ST PAUL'S CATHEDRAL

The first cathedral was built of wood after missionaries arrived to convert the Saxons to Christianity in the 9th century.

THE AMPHITHEATRE

In Alfred's day this may have been used as the town meeting place. The medieval Guildhall was built on exactly the same spot.

LONDON BRIDGE IS FALLING DOWN

In 1013 the Danes took London. The story goes that the Saxon King Aethelred got help from King Olaf of Norway to throw them out. The Danes pelted rocks from London Bridge onto Olaf's ships. Olaf's men tied ropes to the bridge and pulled it and all the Danes into the river.

Despite the city's ever-growing importance, Edward the Confessor, the last Saxon king but one, spent most of his time building a magnificent abbey at Westminster, even further west than Lundenwic. To keep an eye on progress he built himself a palace next door.

Edward died in 1066 and was buried only days after his abbey was completed. A few months later William the Conqueror came over from France to invade England, killed Edward's successor Harold, and had himself crowned at Westminster.

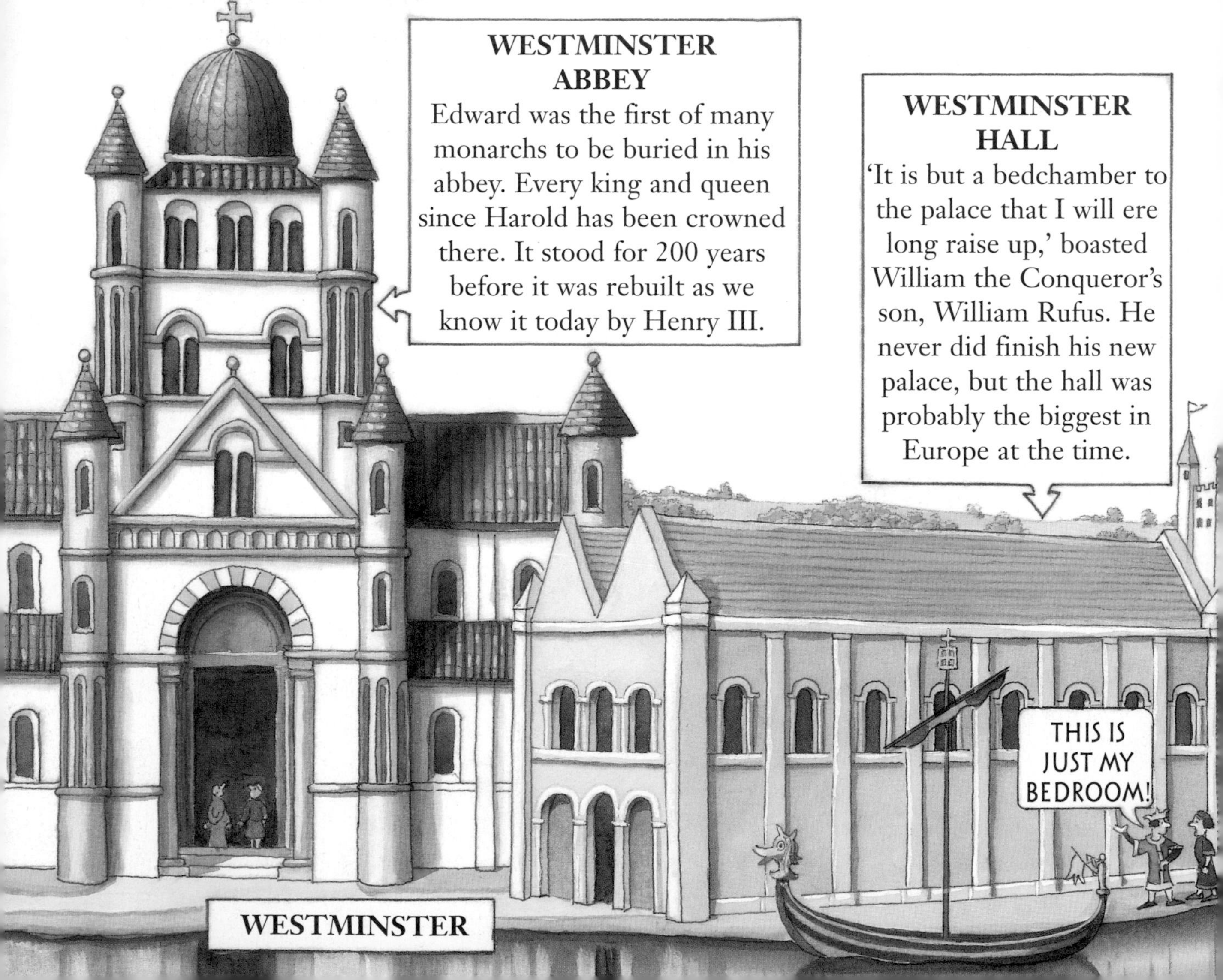

WESTMINSTER ABBEY
Edward was the first of many monarchs to be buried in his abbey. Every king and queen since Harold has been crowned there. It stood for 200 years before it was rebuilt as we know it today by Henry III.
WESTMINSTER HALL
'It is but a bedchamber to the palace that I will ere long raise up,' boasted William the Conqueror's son, William Rufus. He never did finish his new palace, but the hall was probably the biggest in Europe at the time.
THIS IS JUST MY BEDROOM!
WESTMINSTER

To impress the local people William the Conqueror built three castles in the city. One of them was the White Tower, which became the Tower of London. His son William Rufus built a huge hall at Westminster, and work began on a stone cathedral to replace the wooden St Paul's.

The busy City of London was a thousand years old. Now a new centre had sprung up at Westminster. London was all set for the next thousand years.

THE MORTAR IN MY TOWER IS MIXED WITH THE BLOOD OF WILD BEASTS TO MAKE IT STRONG!
WILLIAM THE CONQUEROR 1027-1087
THE CITY
Where LUNDENWIC used to be

ST PAUL'S CATHEDRAL
The wooden cathedral burnt down in the year the Conqueror died. The new stone cathedral went up slowly over the next 200 years. It was longer than the present-day St Paul's and the spire was higher.

THE TOWER OF LONDON
The White Tower, so called after it was whitewashed 200 years later, forms the heart of what is now the Tower of London. As a fortress, a palace, a prison and a treasury, it has been at the heart of British history since it was built.

BAYNARD'S CASTLE AND THE TOWER OF MONTFICHET
William's other two castles disappeared long ago.

THE TOWER OF LONDON

After William completed the White Tower, later kings just kept on adding towers and walls and buildings. All the royal valuables were kept here, and the most important prisoners. One of the last was Hitler's deputy, Rudolf Hess, during World War II.

THE MENAGERIE
This really got going when Henry III was given an elephant and a polar bear. The animals had very little space and people were cruel to them even when they thought they were being kind. The elephant was given gallons of wine to keep it warm. Some ostriches were fed on nails to keep their necks stiff. They didn't last long. But the menagerie lasted until 1835.

THE BLOCK
Only royal prisoners had their heads chopped off in the Tower. Amon them were two of Henry VIII's wives, Anne Boleyn and Catherine Howar

THE MOAT
At one time alligators were kept in the moat. It was drained in 1845.

THE THAMES
The lucky polar bear was allowed to swim in the river and catch fish.

NOT BEEFEATERS
The Yeomen Warders have guarded the Towe since Tudor times. Although they look like th famous Yeomen of the Guard or 'Beefeaters' who guard the monarch, they are not the sam

THE WHITE TOWER
The turrets originally had pointy tops.
THE MARTIN TOWER
It was from here that Captain Blood made his famous attempt to steal the Crown Jewels in 1671.
THE BLOODY TOWER
12-year-old Edward V and his younger brother vanished after their uncle Richard shut them up here. Richard then declared himself king. Two hundred years later the skeletons of two boys were found under the stairs.
THE RAVENS
Legend says the Tower will fall if they ever leave, but their wings are clipped so they can't fly!
GHOSTS
Among the many ghosts are Anne Boleyn, who leads a procession through the chapel, and a large bear which once scared a sentry to death.
HALT! WHO COMES HERE?
THE KEYS.
BETTER SIT HERE THAN IN A WORSE PLACE.
CEREMONY OF THE KEYS
Every night the Tower is locked up and the keys put safely away.
THE TRAITOR'S GATE
Many unhappy prisoners entered through here. When her sister Mary sent her to the Tower, Elizabeth I sat by the river's edge and refused to go in, saying she was no traitor.

During the Middle Ages the City grew into the greatest trading centre in the country. The king had to be careful not to upset the wealthy City merchants. In the twelfth century they were granted their own government, led by the Lord Mayor. It often seemed to rival the king's government at Westminster.

THE CITY GUILDS

IF YOU WANT TO BE A FISHMONGER YOU HAV
TO JOIN OUR GUILD.

To protect their interests, the City tradesmen formed themselves into groups known as Guilds. There were over a hundred, from grocers to goldsmiths to tailors. Many still exist today.

CHARING CROSS

Edward I was mad about his wife Eleanor. When she died outside London in 1290 he built a cross at each place where her coffin rested on the way back. The last cros was on the spot in Trafalgar Square that is now officially the centre of London It was later destroyed, but a replica stands in front of Charing Cross Station

SIR RICHARD WHITTINGTON 1358-1453

Dick came to London in search of streets paved with gold. He didn't find any, and was leaving when the church bells called him back. This may be just a story, but Dick did exist. He became one of the richest merchants in London and was elected Lord Mayor four times – not three, as the bells foretold.

TURN AGAIN WHITTINGTON,
THRICE LORD MAYOR OF LONDON TOWN!

THE BLACK DEATH 1348

Bubonic plague was spread by fleas, which live on rats. After the first outbreak it returned every few years to kill more people. But for every person who died someone new arrived from the country or from abroad to seek their fortune.

By 1348, when the Black Death arrived, there were twice as many people living within the walls as in Roman times. The plague killed about half of them. London would not grow so large again for another two hundred years.

The medieval City had at least a hundred churches and several big monasteries. The church was hugely important in people's lives. It was a meeting place. It told them how to live their lives and it provided education and care for the poor. Merchants such as Dick Whittington left large amounts of money and acres of land to the church. Unfortunately, the church's wealth attracted many dishonest priests.

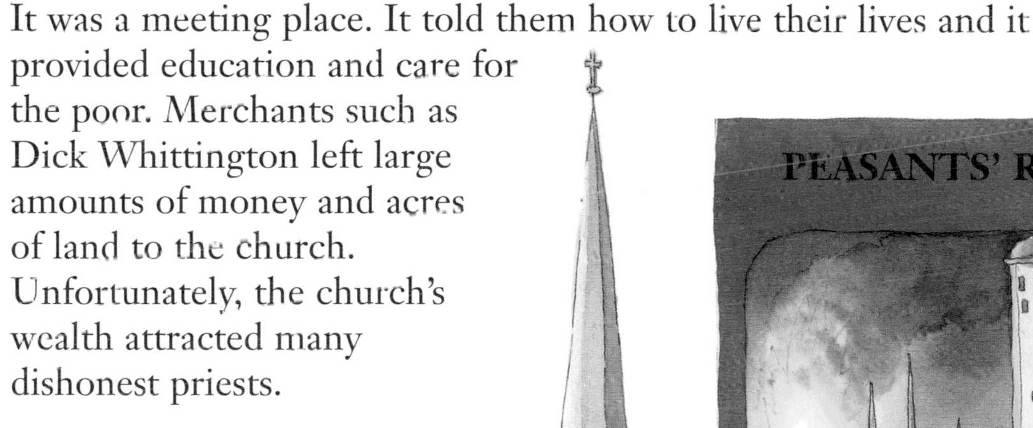

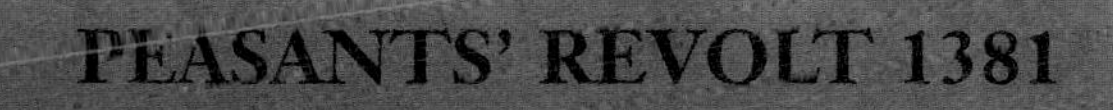

PEASANTS' REVOLT 1381

With so few people left to work the land after the Black Death, the peasants felt they ought to get a better deal. Thousands marched on London, burnt down buildings and broke into the Tower. The king made a number of promises, but soon broke them.

OLD LONDON BRIDGE

Nobody knows for sure what happened to London Bridge after the Romans left. Was it rebuilt or replaced? Did it fall down? Or all of these, several times over? For London to be prosperous it was vitally important to have a bridge that would not fall down.

COME ON!
WHAT'S THE HOLD-UP?
DRAWBRIDG
YIKES!

TRAFFIC
It could take an hour or more to cross.

SHOOTING THE RAPIDS
With so many arches, the bridge acted like a dam. At low tide the water level upstream was often two metres higher than downstream. Passengers in boats usually got off and walked around while the boatman risked his life in the rapids beneath.

AN EVEN OLDER BRIDGE?
It may not have been the Romans wh built the first London Bridge. The remains of oak timbers found at Vauxhall suggest a bridge stood there 1500 years before the Romans arrived

In 1176 construction began on a stone bridge. It had twenty arches and took thirty-two years to build, but it would last for the next 622 years. It was the longest inhabited bridge ever built. At one time there were 138 shops along its length.

GEOFFREY CHAUCER 1340-1400

The son of a London wine merchant, Chaucer was the first poet to be buried in Poets' Corner in Westminster Abbey. In his *Canterbury Tales* the pilgrims set out from the Tabard Inn just south of the bridge.

TRAITORS' HEADS

In 1305 Scottish hero William Wallace's head was stuck on a pole on the Drawbridge Gate. It seemed such a good idea that from then on all traitors' heads were stuck up there.

CHAPEL

I THINK I'LL JUST THROW SOME MONEY AWAY.

CARELESS ROMANS?

In 1832 lots of Roman coins were dredged up from the river bed beside the bridge. Did the Romans think it was lucky to throw coins off their bridge, or were they just careless?

FROST FAIRS

The water behind the bridge often froze solid in cold winters. Shops and stalls were set up and fairs were held on the ice. There was bull-baiting, coach racing, puppet plays, sledding and skating. When the ice began to break up it often pulled an arch or two down with it.

HENRY VIII
1491-1547
By dissolving the monasteries Henry changed the face of London. He was the biggest builder of all, with a huge new palace at Whitehall and many other palaces in and around the city.
When Henry VII, the first Tudor king, came to the throne in 1485 the City and Westminster were still separated by countryside. By 1603, when Queen Elizabeth died, the whole route had been built up. London had four times as many people and was spilling over its walls in every direction.
Henry VIII's decision to get rid of the monasteries meant that all the land they had occupied suddenly became available. There was a mad rush to put up new buildings.
ST JAMES'S PALACE bits still there!
WHITEHALL PALACE There's nothing left of Henry's greatest palace except the wine cellar.
THE TEMPLE where lawyers had their lodgings and still do
BRIDEWELL PALACE nothing left
WESTMINSTER PALACE only the Hall is left
RICHMOND PALACE just a few bricks left
WILLIAM SHAKESPEARE
1564-1616
The theatre became hugely popular in Elizabethan London, but theatres were not allowed within the walls, so they sprang up outside and across the river. Even in his own time Shakespeare was the most famous playwright. He spent most of his adult life in London and was a part-owner of the Globe Theatre.

In 1561 the spire of St Paul's was struck by lightning. It was never repaired.
Elizabethan London exploded with energy. Shipping crammed the Thames, loading and unloading goods. The East India Company was just one of the companies set up to develop trade in newly discovered parts of the world.
JOHN STOW
1525-1605
Most of what we know about Tudor London comes from Stow's *Survey*. The son of a candlemaker, he described the city as it spread in every direction. Even the farm outside Aldgate where he had collected milk as a boy disappeared beneath houses.
THE ROYAL EXCHANGE
Built in 1570, it helped make London a financial centre.
WHERE HAVE ALL THE COWS GONE?
BAYNARD'S CASTLE
all vanished
In 1590 three men were sent to prison for 'riotously behaving at football in Cheapside'.
THE TOWER
still there!
THE GLOBE THEATRE
has been rebuilt
ST OLAVE'S SCHOOL WILL TECHE THE CHELDARNE . . . TO WRETE AND REDE
Local church parishes ran everything from small courts to schools. (Spelling was not a strong point in Tudor times.)
IT'S A VERY WOOD OF TREES . . . SO SHADED IT IS WITH MASTS AND SAILS!
GREENWICH PALACE
all gone

THE GUNPOWDER PLOT 1605

THESE NEW LAWS AGAINST US ARE UNFAIR.

Some Catholics plotted to blow up Parliament with King James inside.

But Guy Fawkes was found in the cellar at Westminster – just in time!

REMEMBER, REMEMBER THE FIFTH OF NOVEMBER!

Guy was tortured and hanged. The king's escape is celebrated each year.

POOH! I'M HEADING WEST.
WE CAN'T AFFORD TO MOVE.

'London is grown too big for the kingdom,' announced a historian at the time of Charles I. Even during the Civil War it just kept growing. By the end of the seventeenth century it was the biggest city in the world. Slums grew up all around the City walls. Richer people moved west in the direction of the wind to escape 'the fumes, steams and stinks'. Despite schemes to provide fresh water, most people still drank straight from the Thames.

MMMM, NICE REFRESHING THAMES WATER. YUCK!

INIGO JONES 1573-1652

Inigo Jones designed the Queen's House at Greenwich, the Banqueting House in Whitehall and St Paul's Church in Covent Garden. Soon everybody was building in the new classical style.

THE QUEEN'S HOUSE
Jones's first design after visiting Italy.

THE BANQUETING HOUSE
After losing the Civil War, Charles I was beheaded on a scaffold outside.

ST PAUL'S CHURCH
The centrepiece of the first great London square.

Ever since the Black Death, plague had broken out every few years. But the Great Plague was something quite different. Twice as many people died as in any previous epidemic. Worst affected were the rat-infested slums.

Nobody paid much attention to the first few cases.

In June numbers grew alarmingly. Anybody who could left town.

As soon as one person in a house caught the plague, everybody else was locked in. They were only allowed out when the cart went by to collect the dead.

It was thought that cats and dogs carried plague. The Lord Mayor ordered them to be killed. A bad move. Cats and dogs helped kill rats.

Thousands of bonfires were lit. People thought the smoke would stop the plague spreading through the air, but it just made everybody cough.

By the end of the year, there were 80,000 dead and London was a smoky ghost town. The king stayed away until February.

Charles II created St James's Park and always walked his rather disobedient spaniels there. The Mall was originally the pitch for his favourite game, pall mall. The Russian ambassador gave him some pelicans for the lake. Their descendants still live there.

SAMUEL PEPYS ('Peeps') 1633-1703

Pepys kept his famous diary throughout the Plague and the Fire. He became Secretary of the Admiralty and often saw the king. He has left us a wonderfully vivid picture of London life.

The Plague and, a year later, the Fire were the two terrible disasters of Charles II's reign. But the city hardly seemed to draw breath as it rushed to get bigger and richer. Charles loved everything about London, especially the theatre and actresses like Nell Gwynne. He got Sir Christopher Wren to design many important buildings. He encouraged the Royal Society, which put London at the cutting edge of scientific progress. And he reformed the Navy which protected the merchant ships that made the city rich.

SIR CHRISTOPHER WREN 1632-1723

Scientist, astronomer and architect. His master plan for rebuilding the City after the Fire was rejected, but 51 churches, St Paul's Cathedral and many other great buildings were completed.

The Great Fire of London destroyed all the medieval City and left 100,000 people homeless.

Many people thought the City was finished, but within five years nearly three-quarters of the houses had been rebuilt. New regulations were brought in. Houses had to be made of brick and streets were widened.

During the eighteenth century London became the first city in the world since ancient Rome to have more than a million people. It was such a bustling chaos that many of them couldn't cope. Drunkenness was a major problem. Business deals were done everywhere, from the new coffee houses to the street. Foreigners who visited were astonished.

WILLIAM HOGARTH 1697-1764

London's greatest painter. His paintings of 18th century London include *A Rake's Progress*, which follows a young man as he wastes his life on the many temptations of the city. His pug dog's name was Trump.

ST JAMES'S PALACE

Amazingly, almost anybody could wander off the street into the king's palace. One such visitor was so busy nosing around that he tripped downstairs and knocked himself out. When he came to, King George II was sticking a plaster on his forehead.

OOOOPS!!!
SIND SIE OK?

GEORGE FREDERICK HANDEL 1685-1759

MAYBE IT'S BECAUSE I'M A LONDONER . . .

The great German composer was crazy about London. He added an 'e' to Georg to make it sound more English, composed his famous *Messiah* at his house in Mayfair, and is buried in Westminster Abbey.

The docks were easily the busiest in the world, the Thames 'almost hidden by merchant vessels from every country'. All this activity created other jobs of every kind. Dealers in shares set up the Stock Exchange. Banks and insurance companies multiplied. The demand for cheap labour never ended.

IGNATIUS SANCHO
1729-1780

Sancho first came to London as a slave, but he wrote music and letters, acted, campaigned against slavery and was the first black person to vote in an election. He also ran a grocery shop near Charing Cross.

With so many people packed together, disease killed more Londoners than were born each year. But immigrants poured in – Scots, Irish, French Protestants, Jews, all kinds of people on East India Company ships and as many as 10,000 of African descent. By about 1750 only one in twenty Londoners had been born there.

THE GREAT EARTHQUAKE SCARE

On 8 April 1750 nearly everybody fled the city after the Bishop of London said it would be destroyed by an earthquake. They waited all day. Nothing happened. So they all went home.

The rich continued to move west into the fine new squares of Mayfair, Bloomsbury and Belgravia, which had until recently been open countryside. The houses they left behind often became slums. To the east, acres of cheap housing grew up around the docks.

DR SAMUEL JOHNSON
1709-1784

The famous writer and compiler of the first English dictionary moved to London as a young man. He thought all the hustle and bustle was so fantastic that he stayed for the rest of his life.

REGENCY LONDON
MADAME TUSSAUD'S
Madame Tussaud opened her wax museum near Baker Street with heads cast from victims of the guillotine in the French Revolution.
REGENT'S PARK
SHOPPING
Many famous West End shops opened at this time. The great novelist Jane Austen shopped till she dropped in Bond Street whenever she came to town.
TYBURN
Hangings at Tyburn were popular events. Jack Shepherd, who escaped from Newgate prison four times, attracted a crowd of 200,000.
IT IS A TRUTH UNIVERSALLY ACKNOWLEDGED THAT I NEED TO SHOP!
OXFORD CIRCUS
BURLINGTON ARCADE
lots of small shops
REGENT STREET
THE DUKE OF WELLINGTON'S HOUSE
BOND STREET
HYDE PARK
PICCADILLY
ST JAMES'S PALACE
IT WON'T FIT, SIRE!
ST JAMES'S PARK
THE MALL
MARBLE ARCH
Nash made the grand entrance to Buckingham Palace too small for the State Coach, so it was pulled down and moved near Tyburn.
FIRE
In 1834 the House of Parliament burnt down.
BUCKINGHAM PALACE

JOHN NASH
1752-1835

Nash's grand design included Regent's Park, Regent Street, Piccadilly Circus and Trafalgar Square. The front of Buckingham Palace and many of his other buildings have since been mucked about.

When George III went mad his son, later George IV, took his place as Prince Regent. With his architect John Nash he entirely reshaped the West End as we know it today.

The defeat of Napoleon at Waterloo in 1815 confirmed London as a world beater. No other city approached it in wealth or population.

HAMLEYS
William Hamley opened his first shop, called Noah's Ark, in 1760 in High Holborn.

THE BRITISH MUSEUM
Founded in 1753. The present building was begun in 1823.

HORNER'S PANORAMA
During repairs to St Paul's in 1821 Thomas Horner painted the city while living in a hut on top of the dome. He nearly got blown off several times.

ST KATHARINE'S DOCK
was just one of many docks dug out beside the Thames so all the thousands of ships could land their cargoes.

TRAFALGAR SQUARE

THE NATIONAL GALLERY
The columns came from one of George IV's palaces which he'd got tired of.

LONDON BRIDGE
was rebuilt in 1831.

WESTMINSTER BRIDGE
Built in 1750. The first new bridge for 700 years.

CRIME

In the 18th century thieves could be hanged for stealing just a few pennies.

There was no real police force before 1749, when the Bow Street Runners were set up in the Covent Garden area.

HANG ON, JOHN!
...GLURP!!

In 1829 Sir Robert Peel created the London-wide Metropolitan Police Force based at Scotland Yard and known as 'Bobbies' or 'Peelers'.

The hangman was often careless. John 'Half-hanged' Smith was just one of several cut down and revived by friends.

QUICK! QUICK! MY DARLINGS

Characters like Fagin in Dickens' *Oliver Twist* gave children food and shelter in return for picking pockets.

CHARLES DICKENS 1812-1870

All Dickens' great novels centre on the rapidly changing city with its 'Dickensian' mix of poverty and wealth. His own life reads like one of his novels. When he was twelve he suddenly had to leave school to work in a factory after his father was imprisoned for debt. He went on to become by far the bestselling author of the age.

During the nineteenth century London's population exploded from one to six million. There had never been such an enormous city or such enormous problems. New methods had to be thought up to deal with the terrible poverty, the crime, the huge amount of pollution and horrendous traffic jams.

CHIMNEY SWEEPS
Until 1829 small children were used to crawl up inside chimneys.

HENRY MAYHEW 1812-1887

Journalist Henry Mayhew peered into every corner of Victorian London and left us an extraordinary picture of what he found . . . toddlers sent out to work and people so poor they'd do almost anything for a few pennies.

London was bursting with life, odd customs and entertainment.

PURE COLLECTORS
Dog messes or 'pure' were used in curing leather!

MUDLARKS
searched the Thames mud for anything they could sell.

CROSSING SWEEPERS
hoped for a tip by sweeping as people crossed the road.

?

THIS HEAP OF COKE WANTS SOME FINGER AND THUMB
(THIS BLOKE WANTS SOME RUM)

Cockneys sometimes spoke rhyming slang.

THE PUNCH AND JUDY MAN
A common sight on street corners

PUNCH

KOOL TUO!
A NAMECILOP!

Costermongers or street sellers used back to front language.

HEADS!
TAILS!

TOSSING THE PIEMAN
If you called correctly, you got a pie and your money back. Incorrectly . . . no pie, no money!

THE PENNY GAFF
There were hundreds of these small theatres. They had dancing and very rude songs.

DR JOHN SNOW 1813-1858

In 1854 Dr Snow noticed that all the victims of a cholera epidemic in Soho drew water from the same well. After he removed the pump handle nobody else got sick.

SEWAGE MUST BE LEAKING INTO THE WELL.

I'LL REMOVE THE HANDLE . . .

. . . AND PROVE IT'S THE CAUSE OF CHOLERA.

One of the greatest problems was sewage flowing straight into the Thames at a time when most people still drank water from the river. It was only gradually accepted that diseases such as cholera and typhoid, which killed thousands each year, were spread in the water.

UGH!

YUCK!
I MOVE THIS HOUSE MOVES . . . QUICKLY!
POOH!

THE GREAT STINK

The Thames had been stinky for years. In the very hot summer of 1858 it became unbearable. The spanking new Houses of Parliament had just opened beside the river but the M.P.s couldn't bear to sit in it. Eventually they gave up and went home, but determined to do something about it.

Eventually, in the late 1850s, a massive scheme was begun to build miles of sewers to collect waste before it reached the river and carry it far enough downstream to flush out to sea.

POOH!
SEWER
TO THE SEA
THAMES

Some things never change. In 1864 a commuter complained in a letter to *The Times* about how late the trains were at London Bridge Station.

London was only able to grow so huge because of new, fast and cheap ways of getting around. In 1829 came the first horse-drawn omnibuses. A few years later the first railway line was built. All today's main lines and stations went up in a spurt between 1838 and 1864. Then in 1863 the first Underground line opened.

ALL LONDONERS LOOK AS IF THEY'RE RUNNING FOR A TRAIN.

OSCAR WILDE
writer and wit

HOVIS

There were tens of thousands of horses in Victorian London. That meant an awful lot of horse manure to clear up!

THE UNDERGROUND

When the Metropolitan Underground opened the passengers sat in open carriages pulled by steam trains. Soon lines headed out in every direction and with electrification in the 1890s deep tube tunnels became possible.

DON'T WORRY, I CAN USUALLY SEE THE SIGNALS AND THE SMOKE'S GOOD FOR YOU!

Many of the better-off were able to move to the suburbs and come in to work daily on the new trains and buses. Those left behind in the centre were not so lucky. A hundred thousand people had their homes torn down to make way for the railways.

RAGGED SCHOOLS

started in 1854 specially for poor ragged children. Classes often had only one teacher for 200 pupils, most of whom left at ten to start work.

SLUMS

In rundown areas, like the East End, houses had whole families crammed into each room.

SHERLOCK HOLMES

People still come looking for the great detective's flat in Baker Street, but Holmes was not a real person. He only existed in the novels of Sir Arthur Conan Doyle

JACK THE RIPPER

In 1888 five young women were horribly murdered in the slums of the East End. Even with 600 policemen on the job, the murderer was never caught. The police tried using bloodhounds but instead of catching the Ripper the dogs turned on the commissioner during training, and chased him right across Tooting Common

For the growing number of educated people with money to spend, London was the cultural centre of the world.

BEATRIX POTTER
Her childhood home backed onto Brompton Cemetery. Recently some familiar names were discovered among those buried there.

GREAT PAINTERS
American painter Whistler often painted the Thames at Chelsea. French Impressionist Monet came over specially to paint the effect of all the smoky chimneys on the light.

THE ALBERT HALL

THE WEST END
Many of the theatres still in use today were built during the 19th century. The West End sparkled with plays by Oscar Wilde and George Bernard Shaw and with the operettas of Gilbert and Sullivan.

NEW MUSEUMS
The profits from the Great Exhibition were used to build the Victoria & Albert, the Natural History and the Science Museums at South Kensington.

THE ALBERT MEMORIAL
shows just how upset Queen Victoria was when her husband died.

THE GREAT EXHIBITION 1851
Designed to show that Britain was brilliant at new inventions, this was housed in the Crystal Palace with its 900,000 panes of glass. Six million people visited. Queen Victoria and her husband Prince Albert went forty-two times. Albert was one of the main organisers. Afterwards the palace was moved to south London and later burnt down.

PETER PAN
The idea for *Peter Pan* came to J M Barrie in Kensington Gardens, where there is now a statue of Peter.

THE HEART OF EMPIRE

By 1911 London had seven million people and was the capital of the biggest empire the world has ever known.

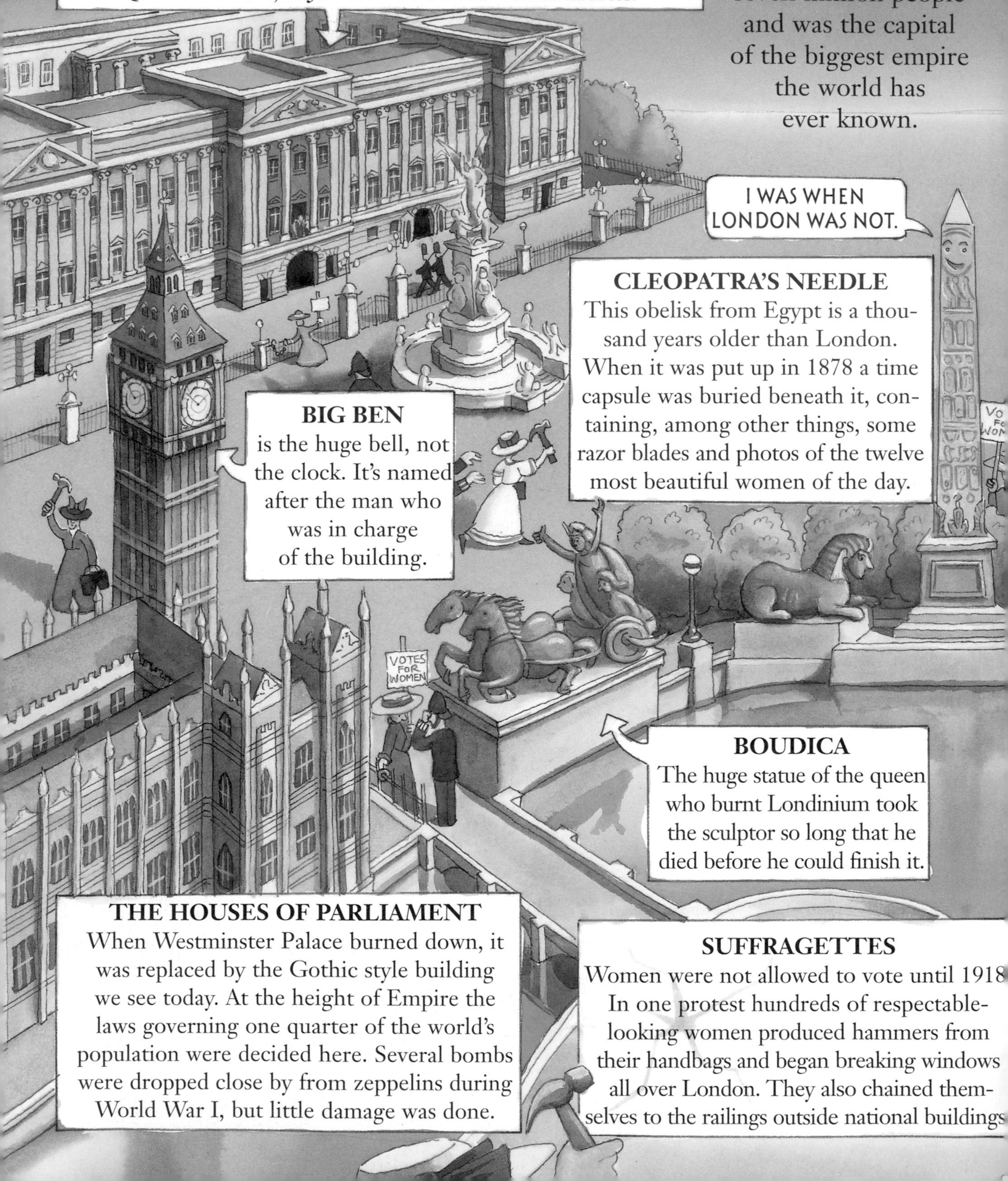

BUCKINGHAM PALACE

Soon after the famous front with its balcony was finished, World War I broke out and a large patriotic crowd gathered outside. Crowds have gathered here on important occasions ever since. Although the Queen lives here, St James's Palace is her official address.

I WAS WHEN LONDON WAS NOT.

CLEOPATRA'S NEEDLE

This obelisk from Egypt is a thousand years older than London. When it was put up in 1878 a time capsule was buried beneath it, containing, among other things, some razor blades and photos of the twelve most beautiful women of the day.

BIG BEN

is the huge bell, not the clock. It's named after the man who was in charge of the building.

VOTES FOR WOMEN

BOUDICA

The huge statue of the queen who burnt Londinium took the sculptor so long that he died before he could finish it.

THE HOUSES OF PARLIAMENT

When Westminster Palace burned down, it was replaced by the Gothic style building we see today. At the height of Empire the laws governing one quarter of the world's population were decided here. Several bombs were dropped close by from zeppelins during World War I, but little damage was done.

SUFFRAGETTES

Women were not allowed to vote until 1918. In one protest hundreds of respectable-looking women produced hammers from their handbags and began breaking windows all over London. They also chained themselves to the railings outside national buildings

By the end of World War I, New York rivalled London as the largest city in the world. But London was still gobbling up the surrounding countryside and growing faster than ever.

DEPARTMENT STORES
YOU CAN BUY ANYTHING HERE!
First Whiteleys, then Harrods, began in the 1860s. In 1909 Selfridges set a new standard in luxury. The others were quickly rebuilt to look like palaces.
WEMBLEY STADIUM
The centre of the British Empire Exhibition in 1924, attended by 27 million people. The F.A. Cup Final was played here until 2000.
MY PHOTO BETTER BE UNDER THERE!
TOWER BRIDGE
Built in 1894 to look medieval, in keeping with the Tower, the bridge soon became one of London's most famous landmarks.
OOPS!
AIR RAIDS
Nearly 700 people were killed by air raids in World War I. An anti-aircraft gun on Tower Bridge shot a hole in the Tower by mistake!

When World War II broke out in 1939, everybody expected London would be bombed immediately. Nothing happened for a year. Then the Blitz began. The worst bombing was in May 1941, especially in the East End. After that things went quiet for a while.
Every night wardens watched on the roof of St Paul's to put out fires. The surrounding area was almost totally destroyed, but the cathedral survived.
THE BLITZ
P.M. Winston Churchill became a familiar figure as he inspected bomb sites.
To escape the bombing many children were sent to live in the countryside with people they had never met before.
UNDERGROUND
Everyone carried gas masks. Some even got their dog one.
Londoners with gardens dug a hole for an Anderson Shelter, a tunnel of corrugated steel covered with earth.
IT'S A BOY! YOU SHOULD CALL HIM WINSTON.
THE CABINET WAR ROOMS
The government often met in a special underground shelter. You can still visit it and even see Churchill's bedroom.
Many took to sleeping and living in Underground stations. Several babies were born there.

Then in 1944 the Germans began sending over flying bombs known as doodlebugs, followed by rocket bombs which were enormously destructive. By the end of the war nearly half of London's houses had been damaged. The job of rebuilding seemed almost superhuman.

But as they had after Boudica, the Great Fire and all the other disasters, Londoners clambered over the wreckage and got on with life. Several events cheered them up – the 1948 Olympic Games, the Festival of Britain and the coronation of Queen Elizabeth II.

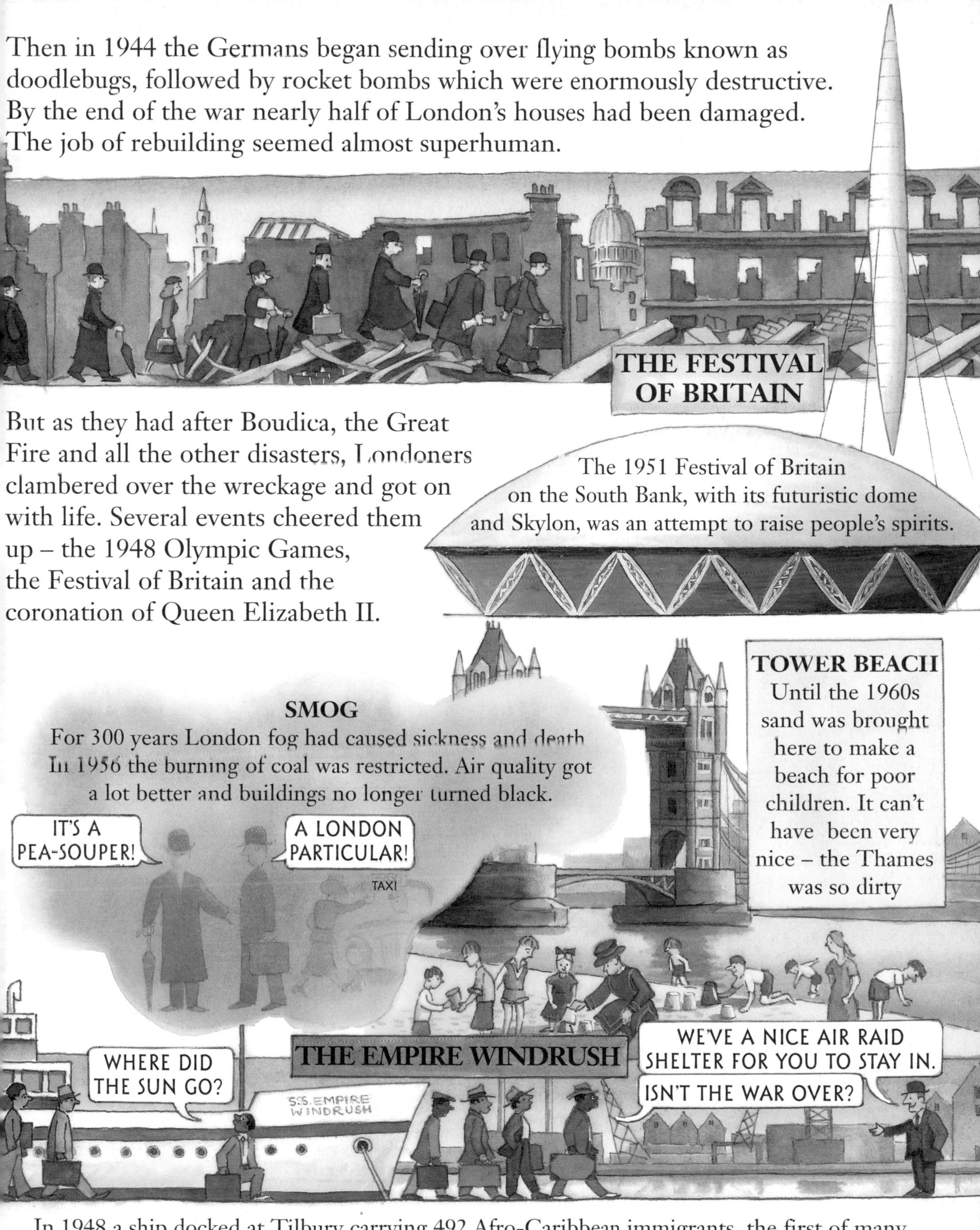

IT'S A PEA-SOUPER!
A LONDON PARTICULAR!
TAXI
WHERE DID THE SUN GO?
S.S. EMPIRE WINDRUSH
WE'VE A NICE AIR RAID SHELTER FOR YOU TO STAY IN.
ISN'T THE WAR OVER?

THE FESTIVAL OF BRITAIN

The 1951 Festival of Britain on the South Bank, with its futuristic dome and Skylon, was an attempt to raise people's spirits.

SMOG

For 300 years London fog had caused sickness and death In 1956 the burning of coal was restricted. Air quality got a lot better and buildings no longer turned black.

TOWER BEACH

Until the 1960s sand was brought here to make a beach for poor children. It can't have been very nice – the Thames was so dirty

THE EMPIRE WINDRUSH

In 1948 a ship docked at Tilbury carrying 492 Afro-Caribbean immigrants, the first of many. They were temporarily housed in an air raid shelter under Clapham Common.

DOCKLANDS

In the 1960s the once mighty docks nearly all closed as more efficient ports opened nearer to the sea. But the 1980s saw London's tallest tower replace the warehouses of Canary Wharf. A bustling new area of the city has since sprung up. The future looks bright for East London, especially with the arrival of the Channel Tunnel railway link.

'THE MANY STEEPLED SKY WHICH MADE OUR CITY FAIR BURIED IN BUILDINGS HIGH IS NOW NO LONGER THERE.'

JOHN BETJEMAN
The Poet Laureate bemoaned the badly designed tower blocks which sprang up in the 1960s. He and others began to try and save old buildings.

After the war most people thought London had got too big. A ring of countryside, known as the Green Belt, was created around the city with no new building allowed in it. Many Londoners moved to new towns outside the Green Belt.

But it didn't stop hundreds of thousands of newcomers arriving, mainly from countries that had once been part of the British Empire. The different races didn't always get on at first. Now their children have grown up as much Londoners as anybody else.

SWINGING LONDON

During the 1960s London seemed to have become the most exciting city in the world, with the Beatles, the miniskirt, and an explosion in art, theatre, music and fashion.

THE SIXTIES ARE FAB.
I'M A DEDICATED FOLLOWER OF FASHION.

HEATHROW AIRPORT

To the west, Heathrow Airport opened in 1946 and soon proved a magnet for new businesses and jobs. It never stops growing. So much trade and so many travellers pass through it that today it is the busiest international airport in the world. Together with London's other airports, it is the new London Bridge.

London is growing again. Each year tens of thousands of Dick Whittingtons arrive in search of streets paved with gold. The old problems still exist, transport is still bad, but prosperity and new laws have improved living conditions for nearly everybody. London is a better place to live than ever before.

300 different first languages are spoken by children in London's schools . . . from Abe to Zulu to French.

One thing is certain. Some time around 2050 London will be celebrating its 2000th birthday as it always has done – by getting on with business.

I WISH IT STILL WOBBLED!
I'M OFF TO THE ROYAL BALLET. HOW ABOUT YOU?
THE ROYAL OPERA
THE ROYAL NATIONAL THEATRE
THE ROYAL PHILHARMONIC

CITY OF CULTURE

The postwar years saw new ballet and theatre companies and new national orchestras. Today the West End has about fifty full-size theatres. On any night of the week you can choose between hundreds of different entertainments. The new millennium has seen a burst of public building – galleries, museums . . . even a footbridge that wobbled when it first opened.

There are so many sights to see in London. The best place to start is at www.londontouristboard.com which has links to all the main attractions.

You will especially want to visit the Museum of London: (www.museumoflondon.org.uk).

BLUE PLAQUES

These mark the houses of the amazing number of famous people who have lived in London at some time in their lives (www.blueplaque.com).

HELP, MY HELMET'S SHRINKING!
NO MATE, IT'S YOUR BRAIN GROWING!

BLACK CABS

It takes a year of exploring on a moped for taxi drivers to learn the streets of London, known as 'doing the knowledge'. Scientists have found that part of their brains seems to grow larger than other people's, from holding so much 'knowledge'!

Nearby, beneath the Guildhall Art Museum, are the remains of the Roman amphitheatre. No other city in the world has seen so many buildings come and go. The amphitheatre gives you a glimpse of one of the earliest to have vanished beneath the ground.

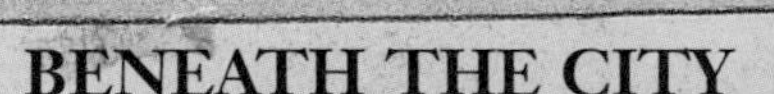

BENEATH THE CITY

A hundred miles of once open rivers now flow through underground tunnels.

London pigeons quite often travel by Underground. You'll see them hop onto a train at one station and hop out at the next, probably looking for food.

Nobody knows for sure, but there may be as many as ten million rats living beneath the city. Luckily the plague-bearing black rat disappeared after the arrival of the fiercer brown rat in the eighteenth century, and the last epidemic was the Great Plague.

IS THIS THE TRAIN FOR TRAFALGAR SQUARE?